Thailand

By Landen Harris

Thailand

by Landen Harris

Printed in the United States of America

ISBN: 978-0-9789265-0-2

Cover Design and Published by Lucid Books

LucidBooks.net

The Preface

If I take the wings of the dawn,
If I dwell in the remotest part of the sea,
Even there Your hand will lead me,
And Your right hand will lay hold of me.

Psalms 139: 9-10

—

Because I prayed
this word:
I want

Sappho

I

June 14th

Curious George ushers in the dawn, but the clock is not needed. I am wide awake, cloaked in covers and fear. I sit up in bed and fold my hands over my baseball pillow. I ask God to forgive me for my sins. I pray for His rain of blessings over this sojourn. I pray for those praying for me. I ask for a chance to die. I ask for wisdom.

—

For one last time I look over my inventory:

Backpack, map, camel pack, three mechanical pencils, two black Moleskins, NKJV Bible, Frommer's Guide To Thailand, Lonely Planet Thai phrase book, Lord of Chaos, airline tickets, black organizer, compass, passport, first-aid pack, six handkerchiefs, black and red athletic shoes, brown flops, heavy carabineer, black swim suit, pictures, two disposable cameras, brown Hollister shorts, gray Texas Tech Baseball shirt, watch, black bracelet, Dodgers baseball cap, face wash sheets, blue nylon shorts, black nylon shorts, gray undershirt, navy undershirt, two white undershirts, two toothbrushes, cinnamon toothpaste, contact case, contact solution, shampoo, conditioner, two hand sanitizer bottles, Dove soap, Kilo, eye-glasses, zip-lock bags, razors, shaving cream, anti-bacterial pills, sun block, Flintstones, flashlight, pirate boxers, kangaroo boxers, Thailand boxers, aviator shades, electronic chess, white sox, black sox, green rain jacket, Altoids, grandmother's peanuts.

I bring my swollen backpack into the living room and sink down onto the couch. I stare at the phantom inside my passport. Harris Clay Landen. 01 Dec 1984. Male. Texas, USA. In the photo his curls are long and chaotic and his eyes are the darkest green.

I stand up and pace. I let out a tiny gray jaguar into pale morning light. I have already said goodbye to Kelsey, gone on a trip of her own. Soon my parents will drive me from Abilene to DFW, where I'll fly to Seoul, then Bangkok. I want to wander the northern mountains, then the southern tropics.

I call April. And I pace.

—

On the road to the airport I listen to my sister's headphones and drink strong coffee. The music echoes my quest's prelude inside my brooding mind.

"Some may say this might be your last farewell ride." — Beck

"I just have to wander through this world alone." — Pete Yorn

"To make or break you down I pray." — Kasabian

"Am I in any danger? Yes I am. Do I like what's happening? Yes I do." — Fischerspooner

"You won't be around forever girl, you gotta' grab life with both hands." — Snow Patrol

"Nineteen—talking in my head got harder to understand." — John Vanderslice

"Can you picture what will be? So limitless and free." — The Doors

"If you're lonely when you sleep at night, I'm sorry that you knew me." — Hope Of The States

"Grant us peace and grant us hope. Christe Elesion." — Michelle Tumes

"Jesus' blood never fails me." — Delirious?

"Agætis Byrjun." — Sigur Rós

—

Mom and dad pray over me in the airport parking lot. I tell them I will come home.

My dad says I know. My mom cries.

—

An Emperial Stormtrooper glowers from the right arm of the guy walking next to me down the gate 44 tunnel.

"Cool ink," I say.

"Thanks man."

June 15th

The sky of Seoul is still ash. Black rain glimmers against the airplane windows, but we take off without delay. As we fly over the Yellow Sea the captain comes on and tells us we are going to rise to fly over an approaching lightning storm.

I feel brave.

I feel haunted.

II

June 16th

I hand the taxi driver a map that shows directions from the airport to Big John's Hostel. He hits the meter and starts speaking in Thai.

"I don't really speak Thai," I say.

He continues talking as he weaves his green and red Honda throughout traffic. Motorbikes crackle past us in the same lanes. Neon 7/11 signs illuminate the girls standing beneath them. The driver turns to me and pauses. I nod. He smiles and keeps talking.

—

At Big John's I take a freezing shower, then walk upstairs to my shared room on the roof. Two Indian girls sleep as a fan rotates between their beds. My watch chimes and I press the glow to read two a.m.

I thank the Lord for His faithfulness.

—

Breakfast at Big John's is two easy eggs, two peppered sausages, two pieces of buttered toast and two cups of coffee with cream and cane sugar. I look up the word for delicious in my Thai phrase book.

"A-roy mahk," I tell the young woman behind the counter.

"Korp kun," she says.

—

I walk without destination. Food vendors and cigarette carts line the hazy streets. Bone cats and bone dogs sleep restlessly or gnaw on discarded squids. The homeless reach out on every corner and under every bridge.

The Bangkok Skytram looms above—a vast aerial serpent that connects all of the city's districts. I buy a one-day pass and take the train to the Chao Phraya River, then buy a ticket on a barge that will take me to The Oriental. But I miss the stop and the barge lets me off at the Royal Palace docks. When I walk near the gates I'm warded away because of the Princess of Thailand. Walking away from the temples an old man grins at me and grabs my arm.

"Hello," he says.

"Hello."

"You Lakers fan?"

"No. This is the Dodgers." He looks confused. "You know... baseball." He looks even more confused. "I tried to go to the Royal Palace but—"

"Princess of Thailand today!"

"Yes."

"May I see you map? I am professor at National University here in Bangkok. I show you good sights to see, yes?"

"Thank you."

He takes out a black pen and begins scribbling symbols on my map.

"You know tuk-tuk?"

"Yes."

"Today Buddhist holiday. All yellow tuk-tuk only twenty baht for hour. You find yellow tuk-tuk and go these places."

"Thank you."

I had taken a few tuk-tuks and they cost around one hundred baht for a short trip. But most tuk-tuks are green, white or red.

"I give you Buddha's blessing of luck. Mmm, yes, yes. Goodbye, I must teach class now, goodbye."

"Goodbye, thank you very much."

I begin down the street again, but during our conversation the Thai guard had blocked the road off. As I walk down another street I see a yellow tuk-tuk zoom around the corner. Before I can raise my hand he screeches to a halt in front of me and smiles wide through his cigarette.

"You need tuk-tuk?"

—

Two black cats rub against my ankles as I gaze up at the world's largest Buddha. At the Emerald Luck Buddha I watch tendrils of silver and pearl incense waft over the chanting. And I stand barefoot in front of the bars that guard the Golden Buddha.

I ponder and I listen.

—

Inside a 7/11 I drip rain and fog as I buy an international calling card. Outside I try several phone booths, but none have the international mark. I hail a taxi and ask him to take me to thc Seafood Market. He hands me a brochure and drives to a sex parlor instead.

"Sea-food Mar-ket," I say.

"Yes, yes. Then food."

"No."

"Yes, yes."

"No."

"Yes, yes, yes."

I give him some baht and walk.

—

At the Seafood Market I have steamed rice with shrimp and crab, then order a coffee and write in my journal until the rain stops. I put my leftovers in a box and begin to walk back to my hostel. A block away from the restaurant a young homeless man with an Irish accent asks me for any help I can give. I give him some baht and my box. He thanks me and falls asleep immediately. I walk on and buy a Pepsi from an old man with a snow Fu-Manchu mustache. He puts the fizzing soda in a plastic bag with ice and keeps the glass bottle himself.

Back at Big John's I see the man himself and his name is no exaggeration. He watches rugby while drinking whisky and eating sugar cookies. I buy a Dark Heineken and two waters and walk up the six stories to the roof. I dangle my feet over the edge and watch Buddhist shrines smolder in the twilight.

June 17th

I awake before sunrise. In America I am a vampire, but here the dawn is familiar. After breakfast I freestyle swim towards the Skytram. I am sitting beneath a behemoth Batman Begins poster, waiting for the crowded train that will take me to the Grand Palace, when the national anthem begins to thunder out over the entire city. Everyone gets off their cell phones and stands attentive. I know that disrespecting King Rama IX or the royal family will land you in jail for fifteen years, so I remove my cap and face burning skyscrapers in the east.

—

The Skytram stop leaves me miles from the Royal Palace and I hail a tuk-tuk to take me the rest of the way. As I walk towards the driver an adolescent rogue darts out from an alley and latches his hands around my black organizer. But inside I have my passport, baht, airline tickets, pictures, compass, pencils and journal, so my grip is ironclad. When he fails he immediately lets go and sprints back into the alley.

The tuk-tuk driver shrugs and pats the seat.

—

All skin must be covered to enter the Royal Palace grounds, so I put on shoes, black socks and my green rain jacket. I'm in my Hollister shorts, so I pull my socks up as high as they can go. The guards let me enter the courtyard, but a woman inside the grounds points to my legs, then points to a small building off to the side of the main gates.

Inside the walls are lined with dark green shirts and pants. Three men and one woman sit at a desk drinking coffee. I take a pair of pants from the stacks and turn back to the four.

"Where do I... ah..."

None speak English, but one man motions to the back of the building. I walk away from them and take my shoes and shorts off. As I'm shaking the pants out I hear a woman screaming. Standing in my kangaroo boxers I turn to see her holding flushed cheeks. The three men look at each other, then explode in laughter. I only understand the Thai word for white.

—

Dynasty after dynasty has built on these sacred grounds. Centuries later the temples are still under construction. The Grand Emerald Palace, champion of the Jade Buddha, is the gold-pillared gem of Thai architecture. I ask a Swiss woman to take my picture before I remove my shoes and step inside the sanctuary. I sit in the back, marveling at the jade sculpture.

Signs are posted on the walls reading: ABSOLUTELY NO PHOTOGRAPHY. PUNISHABLE OFFENSE. But I had already thought of taking a photo of the brilliant carving and the signs only spur me to rebel. I take my camera out of my pocket and turn the flash off. When the guards are not watching I raise the camera.

A grim flash taints the dimness. Startled voices rise up and everyone looks around to find the villain. I slip the camera inside my left sleeve. The guards shuffle around the crowd, but the Jade Buddha casts a new haven and the stillness returns.

—

Near the palace exits, behind a souvenir store, I spy a small ice-cream shop. It is vacant as I enter around midmorning. A shy girl stands behind the counter, reading a book on speaking English. I ask for two scoops of pralines and cream. She gives me three.

"Thank you."

"Very welcome."

—

From the Royal Palace I walk to the Royal Museum. Along the way I meet a Thai man wearing a tuxedo heading the same way. He asks me how long I will be here and I say one month. He asks me if I have enjoyed myself so far and I say very much so. He asks me what I'm going to do while I'm here. I tell him I plan on renting a Jeep and wandering around the northern mountains, then flying to the southern coasts and getting lost by boat. He says that will be very dangerous, but he can tell I have good direction in me. I say thank you.

At the museum gates I pause to pay, but he takes my arm and waves the attendant away. He leads me past a giant shrub elephant, into the main museum. We stand in front of a broken black pillar behind bulletproof glass—an original piece of the first Buddhist wat. He sighs and says something in Thai. When I turn to him he shakes my hand and says goodbye.

I walk around the museum grounds, then sit down at a gazebo and look over my map. I see that the infamous Khao San Road is nearby and I leave to visit the district. On my way there a Malaysian couple stops me and asks for directions to the Royal Palace. I tell them the way, then they ask me where I am from. I say Texas. He asks me if I know Bush. I say no. She asks me if I ride a horse. I say no. They both look disappointed.

—

Tomorrow I leave early for Ayuttaya—the original capitol of Siam from 1350 until the Burmese sacked the city in 1767. In the north I'll have to eat many vegetables and fruits, so I should prepare my body before. This could be a struggle since the only vegetable I eat is fried okra and the only fruit I eat is bananas. For remedy I sit down in a back alley of Khao San Road and order black sticky rice with coconut milk and bananas. I'm going to ease into this. I'm not worried though, I have my Flintstones.

—

In my room I find the two Indian girls have moved out and one new girl has moved in. Her clothes and covers lie on a gray and baby blue backpack with a French flag patched on the side. I plug in the fan between us and lay down.

I ask the Lord to give righteous action to my mind. I pray to know the darkness and the light. I ask to see a tiger. I ask for wisdom.

June 18th

The jagged Bangkok skyline is a volcano of pink and purple lava. At the railway station I buy a third-class ticket to Ayuttaya and a second-class sleeper ticket to Chiang Mai. They tell me they will give me half off if I take a top bunk. I was going to request one.

Waiting outside the train station I see an ancient monk and find 'Can I take your picture?' in my phrase book. I read it to him, but give a terrible translation and he does not understand. Handing him the book, I point to the line.

"Ah," he says. "Yes, yes."

—

In Ayuttaya I have six hours before my sleeper to Chiang Mai leaves. I look at a map of the city and one wat immediately captures my imagination—Wat Chaiwattanaram, once the Grand Palace of Siam.

There are no tuk-tuks here, but a truck driver offers to take me there for eighty baht. After we arrive he asks me if I want him to wait. I ask how much and he says eight hundred baht. I tell him goodbye. He says I will be stuck here forever.

—

Wat Chaiwattanaram is haunted. The fallen capitol still touches the sky centuries after its collapse. I climb the tallest tower to look out over miles of unadulterated green. I see legions of Burmese warriors—cutting the heads off Buddhist statues, shooting flaming arrows at Siam defenders and screaming battle chants through bronze demon masks.

A school bus arrives and bubbles out pink-clad Thai boys and girls. I watch them sprint for the highest tower. They race up the worn stone steps to become legends. The adults gather below and take out cameras. I rise to leave, but the children grab onto my limbs and tug me back down.

I pray I will always be a child.

—

I sit under the shade of a somber tree and wait for my path to be revealed. For two hours only school buses arrive, then a white van pulls into the parking lot. Four college girls and one boy get out and walk to the ruins. The driver sits down under my tree. He lights a cigarette and we begin to talk. He tells me about the history of Wat Chaiwattanaram. He tells me the Burmese didn't fully conquer Thailand and that only Thailand and the United States have never been taken over. He asks me if I knew that. I say no, I didn't. When he asks me what I'm doing now I tell him I'm stranded and he insists I come with them.

As we drive back into town one of the girls tells me they are seeing southeast Asia with guides. I tell them I am wandering Thailand alone. They are driving to Bangkok, but they let me out at a park close to the railroad station. As I'm leaving the driver gives me a bottle of OFF and the college kids tell me they are scared for me out here—going into the wild by myself and with only a backpack. I tell them I am too.

—

Gold and ruby elephants lumber up and down the park streets. They are gentle and unharnessed, slowly stomping behind their masters. As I walk through the park I come across a group of vendors. I buy two waters, drink one and refill my camel pack with the other.

At the last tent a toothless man sells blades of all kinds, from daggers and swords to scythes and machetes. I find what I want to take with me on my trek—a sharp on top, serrated on bottom, eight inch blade in a black leather sheathe.

—

A wooden pavilion crumbles next to a barren water fountain on the outskirts of the Chiang Mai park. Six young boys on rusted tricycles chase skeleton dogs around the cracked marble. I sit down on the edge of the pavilion. The youngest of the six hides at the other end and watches me. I look over my maps, then begin to hear the softest steps. I turn around to see the advancing boy freeze, several feet from the edge. When I look away he comes closer and closer, until finally swinging his legs over beside me. He gazes up at me with bright chocolate eyes. I take out my tin of Altoids and offer him one. He only stares. I take a green one and eat it and he does the same. I take a red one and he does the same. I take a white one and he does the same. He smiles with curiosity and begins to rummage through my things, touching and shaking everything he can find. He holds up my new blade before himself like a mastersword.

A ruckus sounds from behind and I see his friends stampeding towards us. They surround us and I offer them some mints. They all reach without hesitation, taking fistfuls. Then the oldest one grabs the entire tin and runs away. They all follow save my friend. When they realize he has not come with them two rush back and begin pulling him away.

"Wait," I say, holding up my camera.

The children all recognize the object and leap together into frame. I take a photo, then wave as they run across a dry creek. My little friend still struggles, but I throw him a thumbs up sign. He smiles and returns the gesture with both hands held high.

—

Pacing the streets around the train station I meet a man from Japan from Boston named Doug. Neither of us have eaten so we sit down at an outdoor restaurant. I order a Pepsi and something he suggests. Doug tells me he has been living in the east since he got out of college in the 60's. He asks me what I'm doing in Thailand and I say just wandering around. He tells me that is inspiring because he has no faith in youth today. I say I don't either. He notices my L.A. cap and we start talking about baseball. He asks me if I think the Dodgers will win the World Series. I say no, I think the Rangers or White Sox will. He says he just wants anyone but the Yankees to win. I raise my Pepsi in toast.

June 19th

Morning starlight is accompanied by a young Thai boy, holding an ice-bucket of orange juice and screaming "Yuce! Yuce!" as he skips down the rocking train. In Chiang Mai I am bombarded by tuk-tuks and taxis outside, but I walk past them. I have looked over my map and on the way to my hostel there is a church I want to visit.

Underneath oily heat my turtle shell grows heavy against my spine and I soon become lost. A monk sees me sitting on a bench with my creased map outstretched and sits down next to me.

"Where go?"
I show him on the map.
"Ah," he says, pointing. "You see bridge."
"Thank you."

He gathers his frayed orange robe and floats away.

I go in the direction he said and find the group of buildings I'm searching for, but all the signs are in Thai and there are guards at every door. On the map the legend shows the Christian church is next to three Muslim, three Buddhist and one Hindu. None of the guards watch me with invitation. I walk on until I find the bridge the monk spoke of. I sit down next to the Ping River and read Ecclesiastes. Solomon tells me the end is better than the beginning.

I have always believed him.

—

Sarah hands me my room key and I'm heading for the stairs when a mammoth golden retriever runs out from under a table. He leaps on me and slobbers as I scratch his caramel ears. She claps her hands and he jumps down. Two muddy paws mark my gray shirt.

"I'm so sorry," she says.

"No, no, it's fine. I love goldens. I have one myself."

"He doesn't behave very well."

"Good, neither does mine."

—

I throw my backpack down onto the bed and my watch almost slips off my wrist. I tighten the band to the last notch. Since the wilderness is close I should eat a grand meal. In Frommer's I find an Italian wood-oven pizzeria.

At the restaurant a girl sits me outside where I can see the wood-oven and smell the rich herbs and spices. I hear the occasional shout of Italian or Thai as I look over the menu. I order a large pepperoni with extra cheese and two cream soda shakes.

I ask for a paper and she brings me the English-version of the Chiang Mai paper. I read baseball statistics until the arrival of a culinary masterpiece. I start to cover the pizza in Parmesan as I usually do, but cannot. I close my eyes and take a bite. A word comes out of my mouth. Italian maybe. Thai maybe. I could have even made it up. But whatever I said it meant that this pizza was the best pizza I had ever tasted.

—

At night I make my way to the Chiang Mai night bazaar. I walk up and down miles of tables, galleries and booths. It begins to rain, but the bartering does not damper. The sellers raise plastic sheets over their wares and continue on. The first item I buy is a fake black and blue North Face single-strap backpack. I pray for discernment and walk out into the rain.

—

I drink a pot of Earl Gray at a cove below ground and think about what tomorrow brings. At noon my 4x4 should arrive and I could sail away into the green unknown.

May the Lord always guide my footsteps.

June 20th

The truck arrives exactly on time. A stout, dark gray, right-hand drive, 4x4 Suzuki with five-speed transmission and a straight six. After handing over 12,000 baht and a copy of my passport I am given the keys and a warning of the truck's quirks—refill the water everyday, keep an eye on the oil, rain will come through when it storms, radio and a/c do not work. They give it to me on E. I fill the tank, then find the main street and drive east. When I come to the highway intersection I race northwards into the rising scape.

In the afternoon moss spheres cascade against my window and burst into fog. Warm rain drips over my toes and onto the pedals. Another major intersection emerges and I look for the direction signs. The main road goes to Mae Hong Song, but as this exit nears a black dog lies down in the street. I swerve and set myself straight for the northern way. I can turn around in a dirt lot, but do not.

The uneven road shrinks to one lane and the barriers rot into the forest below. After several miles I take a left, but this dirt road becomes steep and raw as it cuts into the crest of a mountain. I cannot see the ground below through the treetops.

Mud sludges beneath my tires and I begin to stall, then slide backwards. I shift down to second, then first and still I slide. I hit the brakes, but the truck turns sharply and careens towards the edge. I stomp the clutch and put it in reverse and turn the wheel hard—I have no idea which way. I am aware my mouth is wide open.

I come to a crooked stop in the middle of the road. A motorbike's solo light cuts through the pouring rain. The man is wearing a helmet, but the woman scowls as her husband is forced to go around near the edge. I try to give them a wave.

I crawl back down the mountain and begin to turn right, then pause and listen to the tropical lyre. I go left—into the blank spaces on the map.

—

I stop at a National Waterfall and Park, put on my green rain jacket and run into the main building. It is vacant, save two girls who stare at me and whisper. I look for something to eat, but find nothing. Walking around the lobby one of the girls says something to me in Thai, then kisses the girl beside her on the mouth.

"Sorry," I say. "I don't speak Thai."

—

The road splits into a V. There are no signs anywhere.

Left. Definitely left.

—

The compass points N/NW. I haven't seen another person for hours. In fading dusk I make out a sign that doesn't look like all the previous signs. I have crossed into Laos or Burma. I press my brakes as I near a jut in the mountainside. As I'm turning around the rocks clear and I watch guerillas inhaling cigarettes next to a battered gray long Jeep on the side of the road. When the men see me they yell and gather their guns. I am already spurring the gray beast for glory. One, two, three—I see them in my mirror. Four. I cannot stay on these mountain passes in fifth.

Ahead I see a sign in Thai.

—

The sky is an ethereal door. I count four shooting stars and save all my wishes. A sage appears in my headlights and I pull over to ask him where I am, but he speaks only Thai. I show him the map, but he will only point down a narrow red road, into the belly of the tallest mountain.

I drive down this path and discover a timeless realm. Wooden houses sit atop emerald hills and speckled chickens and filthy hogs run about wild. A shallow river borders the mountain people from the rain forests.

Everyone comes out of their homes as I park. Naked children rush up and touch me. The elders push through and give welcome, graciously leading me beneath covered tables. They bring me a Temple of Doom style feast—eggs, rice and a soup of spiders and brown vegetables. Everyone talks at once, but we have no way to communicate. I get my phrase book out of my backpack and a girl my own age snatches the book from my hand. Several other girls gather around her and they say words in slow English, then laugh. The aroma of burning marshmallows sweetens the air and I see several young men smoking weed nearby.

I write in my journal, then pace near the river bank. Lightning bugs flicker in the darkness—thousands upon thousands, composing an epic chemical symphony. A little girl skips by holding a gray kitten. She disappears into the sole brick building on the shore where everyone is smoking and singing and dancing. The chief's wife walks down next to me and offers her hand out with a wrapped gift.

"Fin?"

Opium.

I say thank you and take the flower.

—

Inside the river house the little girl dances over and hands me her friend, then does not let go of my finger as she stands next to me. The kitten climbs up my shirt and falls asleep on my shoulder. Together we listen to forgotten hymns.

June 21st

Before dawn I walk barefoot alongside the river. I ponder and pray and take photos of the fog hovering over the mountaintops. Only the chief's wife is awake when I come back to leave. I get inside my truck and wave to her and she smiles and waves back. I press the clutch and turn the key.

The engine does not start.

—

The chief's wife and a boy argue as a damask globe burns between charcoal peaks. With gestures I had explained to her that my truck would not start, then she had vanished. When she came back up the road she was talking with this young man. I think she wants him to do something and he certainly does not want to do it. They debate until it seems the wife has won. The boy stomps off and she smiles at me and nods.

When he comes back he is riding an antique motorbike that chugs out black smoke as he accelerates. I jump on the back and he takes off—not towards the road, but towards the rain forest. We speed down the muddy river bank until the engine sputters and stops. He motions for me to get off, then starts running with the bike. The motor roars for short bouts, then gurgles dead. He runs farther and farther away until I can't see him anymore. Then I hear the engine and the boy reappears down the shoreline. He motions for me to leap on as he nears. We ride for half an hour, into the teeth of the rain forest. We tear through ponds and roots and webs. I see leeches hanging from trees and spots of color everywhere. I watch for a tiger.

The hum of running water crescendos and the boy kills the bike and lays it down in the grass. He motions for me to follow him. A small stream appears, with a bridge that curves around the mountainside. The bridge is covered in mushrooms—bruised ivory on top and sparkling lavender beneath. The ropes are frayed and torn. He turns back to me once more, sighs, then steps onto the bridge.

Around the bend I see boundless fields of opium and marijuana. Nearby there is a three-walled house. Inside I see several armed men sitting around smoking. One carves a piece of teak with a long blade. They all stand as the boy rushes up. Their hands drift to holsters. Two have rifles, but the boss that rises to meet the boy has no gun. He walks boldly down the steps of the building. A gold medallion hangs around his neck and an ornate scimitar rests in a jeweled scabbard on his belt.

The boss and the boy begin to argue. The short conversation ends with boy sprinting back towards the bridge.

He does not look at me as he runs by. The boss studies me intently along with all his other men. I notice a woman then, peeking out from a kitchen in the back.

"Come," the boss says. I follow him up the steps and sit down at a wooden round table. Six men stand with guns and stare at me. The boss rests a wrist atop his sword hilt and rubs his chin.

"So... you... American?"

"Yes."

"Mm... mmm... so... you... like... coffee?"

"Yes, please."

He speaks something in Thai to the woman and she brings out a cup.

"Sugar?"

"Milk, please."

If I die, I'm dying with a good cup of coffee. He speaks again to the woman and she brings out a pitcher of cold milk. I pour in the milk and take a drink. Everyone watches my hand rise and fall.

"A-roy," I say. No one speaks.

When I am done the boss asks me, "More?"

"Please."

The woman refills my cup, looking into my eyes for the first time. I drink the second cup and when I finish the boss walks behind me and puts his hand on my shoulder.

"You... you okay."

Immediately everyone begins to laugh and talk at ease. The men sit back down and light up leaves again. The boss rises when the woman brings several blue bowls to a long stone table beside us.

"You have... breakfast... with us?"
"Yes, thank you."

They give me the seat of honor—to the right of the boss at the head of the table. In the blue bowls are rice and beef, but the scent of the beef is so spicy it makes my eyes well. So I drink water and eat only rice until the boss notices I'm not eating any meat. He puts several strips on my plate and waves his hands, saying, "Eat, eat. No spicy, no spicy."

I take a bite and my eyes flood with tears. He smiles at me with his mouth full.

"See? No spicy, no spicy."

I blink through blurred vision.

"Yea—no—spicy."

I drink glass after glass of water. I'm covering a chunk of meat in steamed rice, preparing for another bite, when I see a fist-sized camel and tan spider descend from the ceiling, onto the boss' arm.

"Ah... sir..." I point to the spider.
"Bah." The boss smacks the spider like a gnat and continues eating. The spider balls up on the ground, then flips back onto eight legs and scrambles towards my flops. The arachnid darts up my bare leg and onto my shorts.

"Bah," I repeat, slapping the spider away. The broken creature limps off into the jungle.

The boss nods approvingly and refills my water glass.

—

We follow the boss to a secret shed, covered with thick leaves and branches. They move everything away, revealing a metal cubby cut in the side of the mountain. Inside is a brand new silver Toyota 4x4. I get in the passenger seat and the men hop in the back. The boss shifts into four-low and tramples down the jungle. We emerge next to the river and he follows the current until we get back to the village.

The boss parks next to my truck and motions for me to open the hood and try to start the engine. All the villagers gather to see what will happen. He looks at the gears a long time, does something I cannot see, then holds out his hand for the keys. He gets inside and yells in Thai and his men and I push the truck. I hear something snap, then the engine starts. He revs the motor and drives around us in a circle. Everyone is cheering.

—

I roll down my window and wave farewell as I drive down the red road. The children laugh and shout as they run behind the truck. The smugglers are at the end of the road. They smoke and wave and say good luck. At the very end is the boss.

"See you again," he says.

"Thank you," I say. "Thank you very much."

"Yes, yes," he says. "See you again. See you again."

—

I hit the steering wheel and scream. My cup is overflowing with thankfulness. Thoughts and dawn blind me and I hit a yak on the road. I stop to take a picture of him and check for damage, but there is none. The yak huffs and trudges away.

I stumble upon Chiang Saen and check into the River Hill Hotel. Across the street from the hotel a frail woman runs a bar and laundry. I give her my dirty clothes and write in my journal while I drink scotch.

I notice something on my legs. Mosquito bites. Three on each knee. I think about granddaddy's malaria stories—near death, packed in ice and alcohol with delirious fever.

"People Need The Lord" begins to crackle over the bar radio.

June 22nd

In the morning I drive south to Chiang Rai. The way is narrow and winding and overgrown with reaching, gnarled limbs. In the city I turn towards a mountain range, following a sign that marks waterfalls and hot springs. I drive until I come to a cross in the road. The left goes to the waterfalls and hot springs. The right goes to THE VALLEY OF PEACE. I turn right.

This road elevates up a blue-green mountain. I thought the valley would come before reaching the mountain, but the dirt and rock road leads straight into it. Soon I can only hear the cacophony of the rain forest over second gear. Rain falls and mud oozes up from the cracks in the

Earth. I shift to four-low when I begin to slide. I can never go back.

The 4x4 charges up the mountain until the sides close in and the road abruptly ends. I get out and find a hidden path that continues towards the top. I soak myself in OFF, then lock the truck and begin to walk up the fading way. I feel doomed, but I always do, so I keep climbing. As I near the peak I see a ghost in the distance—something white in all the green and brown and black. Sweat rolls off my legs and back as I reach towards the vision.

Grand white steps appear, leading up to a gold and ivory Buddhist monastery. I ascend the stairway, noticing garden tools and sacks of planting soil lying out. It appears as if they stopped right in the middle of working. Inside the temple I am unnaturally cold despite the scorching heat. The entire place is abandoned, but there are no skeletons or cobwebs. Half-eaten food is out and burning incense dwindles beside the shrines. The prayer mats are still on the floor.
I walk around the complex and find nothing, but I see a crevice in the mountain wall that leads into the peak's heart. I walk down the ivory steps towards the alcove.

Out of shadow he appears. A beautiful sable snake, staring beyond my eyes. He does not move or hiss and I do not move or breathe. After eternity the serpent bows and slithers into the grass.

—

Inside the secret peak I see a brook on the other side. My blood is searing near the flesh, but freezing against the marrow. I am wreathed in shadows. I sense something behind me and turn around. A woman looks straight at me—

but cannot. Her right eye is gone and her left eye is a rotting pulp outside her socket.

She leans forward and whispers. I cannot understand the words. Then she turns around and across her back is a dead baby in a dark orange sash. She shuffles her feet slowly away, not down the road, but into the darkness of the jungle.

I pray to fear nothing save the Lord.

—

My body speeds towards Phayao. My foot is as far down as it can go when I notice the driver of a blue eighteen-wheeler is honking and waving at me.

It is the boss.

—

In Phayao I'm about to stop for the night in a vacant hospital parking lot when I see the Tharan Thong Hotel. I feel like I should check there and I go inside to ask about rooms. The woman at the desk tells me rooms are 660 baht. I say no thank you and turn to go back to the hospital. As I'm walking away she says I can stay for 150 baht.

I put my backpack in my room, then walk down to the market. At a grocery store I buy a liter of Uht sweet milk and a pack of rolls. The milk tastes like frosting.

Back in my room I spread my maps out over the bed. Tomorrow I'll head to Phitsanulok and perhaps further. As I look over the ink roads my mind drifts to THE VALLEY OF PEACE. I dwell upon words I can never remember. Soon I am full of fear and the light flickers off. I pray to be a servant of the Lord forever. The light comes back on.

I do not sleep.

June 23rd

In Phitsanulok I cash in the last of my traveler's checks, then head east towards Lom Sak, but I become lost and find myself driving somewhere near the outskirts of Phetchabun. I look for dinner in a town where there are no signs anywhere. A festival is going on and everyone is parading down the streets with sparklers and liquor. I pull into a dirt lot next to an outdoor café. A young woman comes out who speaks no English and I think she says she will just make me something good. Everyone who walks by talks to me as I wait. Only one Thai police officer knows English. He tells me where I am and marks it on my map. Bantiv.

After three hours the woman comes out with a steaming plate of seafood—shrimp, lobster, crab, scallops, rice and vegetables. I eat every bite, then watch children shoot firecrackers in the streets.

—

Khon Kaen calls. My tank is only a third full, but I think there will be a gas station somewhere in the mountains. I am wrong and the truck dies before the needle even hits the empty slash. So I stand in the jungle black next to my truck, waving a flashlight and counting the cars that go by.

The twentieth stops. A woman in a tiny blue truck

beckons me to get in. She doesn't speak English, but she understands I'm out of gas. As she is driving she points to nursing scrubs in the back, then gives me a cherry energy drink from her cooler. We drive forty minutes out of the mountains, then reach a small town and stop at the house of someone she knows. We borrow a jug and fill it up, then drive back into the mountains.

Before she leaves I try to give her baht, but she refuses. Then I offer her the present I bought for my mom—an onyx sphere with a carved coral soap flower inside. She takes the sphere and hugs me, then writes a number down on a scrap of blue hospital paper.

—

I arrive in Khon Kaen at three a.m. and stop at the first hotel I can find. At the front desk a woman gives me a key to a room on the fourth floor and waves goodbye. I think I am lucky, but after a few minutes there is a knock. A Thai boy is standing there trying to get me to follow him. He leads me downstairs to a pulsating black-glassed room in the basement. He opens the doors for me and I step inside and sigh.

Throbbing techno vibrates the floor as a projector plays porn over a cream wall. School-aged girls sit in booths around the room with porcelain faces and hollow eyes. There are no other guys, save the one who brought me here. The girl behind the bar comes out and takes my arm. She is the youngest of them all.

"Sit, sit," she says. "Any you want. Any you want. What you like drink?"

"Ah... um... water please."

"Water? All right, I get it sir." She leans closer. "I

too... I too," she says, then disappears behind the bar.

I walk out the black doors and go to get my backpack. As I'm leaving the lobby I see the boy again. He laughs like I got lost and waves for me to follow him back. I throw him the room key.

I sleep with the eighteen-wheelers on the highway.

June 24th

I fill up at the gas station with the green dinosaur emblem. After a breakfast of frosting milk and noodles I travel north, past Udon Thani, to Nong Khai—a sleepy town that lies across the Mekong River from Laos.

I drive to the buildings against the shore and find a three-story house with a sign that reads: Coffee / Room. The balconies overflow with flowers and ivy that hang down to stained glass front doors. When I step up to the doors they are locked and the lights are off inside.

I pace through sprinkling mist and find a pavilion near the river where I order rice and shrimp. The fishermen smoke cigarettes and yawn against the tide. When I come back to the river house there are two women sitting inside drinking coffee. I try the door, but it is still locked. One of the women rises and comes to open the door. She shakes my hand and tells me her name is Rose. She leads me to the bar and asks if I would like any coffee or whisky. I ask for coffee and tell her I'd also like a room. Rose apologizes and says the sign is old and she doesn't rent the room out any longer because her friend stays with her now. But then she says her friend is leaving soon and asks me to wait. Rose sits with her friend and they talk while my coffee brews. When Rose brings me my cup she tells me her friend is leaving tonight and she is leaving for Germany next week, but I can stay until then. And she says she will do all my laundry and I can use her computer.

When I finish my drink Rose leads me upstairs. A magnificent oaken bed and branch shelves are carved directly out of the wooden walls of the second story. Sliding glass doors open to the garden balcony I had seen earlier. The deep bells of a wat bellow outside as I wonder what is on the third floor.

—

At the top of the staircase is a hallway with a ceiling much lower than the other two. An intricately carved darkwood door looms at the end. The floor is covered in layers of dust, save a woman's footprints and the handle. I try to open the door, but it is locked.

—

I left the house to buy water and when I returned the doors were locked again. Rose gave me a key, but I hadn't thought I would need it and I couldn't knock because before leaving Rose said she had a headache and was going to take a nap. So I sit my water bottle down and begin to climb up the ivy. The vines hold until my right hand touches the second story balcony, then I hear an organic rip as I plummet.

My watch splinters and shatters beneath me. I lie breathless on my back, slowly bringing back the shards. I limp towards the docks and lean against a slab of worn concrete. A crimson pool grows below my feet as the sun seeps into the river.

I need to be broken.

June 25th

In the morning Rose brings bold coffee and a breakfast of sausage, syrup, eggs, toast and vegetables. I lounge about barefoot—listening to the rain, playing chess, reading, watching the Rangers on the internet and walking near the Mekong.

In the afternoon I travel to a bazaar. A bearded Muslim man, donning a lich hat and carrying a black briefcase, watches me and follows from afar. I stop and stare at him and he walks away, but keeps following when he thinks I do not know. I leave him in the bazaar, then sit down at an outdoor restaurant I had eaten at the day before. A young girl brings me a Pepsi and a water. The Muslim appears and sits down at the table next to me. He opens his briefcase and presses something silver inside, then snaps the case shut. Two steps and he is next to me. He offers a prayer in his birth language.

If this is the end... I'm all right with that.

—

I collapse onto my bed, weeping and worshiping at the foot of the Throne.

I know nothing.

June 26th

I wake up feeling loved and hungry. I find e-mails from my parents and grandparents telling me I'm heavy on their hearts and asking me to let them know I'm safe as soon as possible. After breakfast at The Danish Baker I sit on Rose's balcony with my Bible and the darkest coffee.

Jesus says I need only ask.

June 27th

Rival monks glare at one another as they pace the offering streets at dawn. I drink orange juice and write in my journal inside the nameless restaurant open at four a.m. This day will be my last among the graces of Nong Khai.

—

Rose cries and hugs me and tells me I must come visit her again.

I tell her I will.

June 28th

The darkness drops again as I navigate the mountains, looking for a place to park my bed. Twenty k/m north of Tak I find an abandoned lake, hidden behind a fortress of dying trees. A warped dock leads out to a decaying rowboat. I park, then walk out to the vessel. As I near I see the boat is covered with webs. I rock the boat with my foot and a kingdom of spiders scuttle out from their lairs. Then the smaller spiders disperse as a greater shadow rises. A Queen crawls forward and stands expecting to be worshiped. She has bright yellow and red scales over her molted black-gray body. I hear a low chittering, then she launches herself at me, missing and hitting the water. She glides swiftly back towards the boat. I take a picture, then walk back to my truck.

I sleep under a dead tree.

June 29th

In Chiang Mai I buy a waterproof camera and a peach soap flower in a mahogany sphere to replace the gift for my mom. Walking from the bazaar back to my hostel a ghastly thin Thai man stops me on the sidewalk and points to my Texas Tech Baseball shirt. He yells "Baseball! Baseball!" and shows me his exaggerated Hideo Nomo windup. I nod yes and we hurl our best pitches from invisible mounds.

We throw perfect games.

Interlude

June 30th

In the Bangkok airport I meet two gentlemen from The University of Boston. I'm wearing a green soccer jersey with a clover I bought at the night bazaars. One of the guys asks me if I know what country the jersey is from. I say Ireland. He tells me it is the Greek soccer team. He says he is a fan and has family there.

The three of us sit in freezing terminal seats and drink Guinness and eat chicken nuggets and talk about sports and literature. The soccer guy gives me The Alchemist. He says it is his favorite book and he always buys one when he travels to give to someone. I read it on the flight and offer it back to him when we land, but he tells me to give it to someone else.

—

In Phuket I stay at a hotel that has a morning shuttle to the Koh Phi-Phi launch docks. The owner tells me the islands are all nearly empty. He says this is because of the tsunami and also because it is monsoon season. When he hands me the room key he says be very careful on the islands. The storms are coming.

IV

July 1st

Phuket smalls away inside my ferry window. I put my contacts in for snorkeling at Phi-Phi Le's Maya Beach. The two small islands, Phi-Phi Le and Phi-Phi Don, next to the main island Koh Phi-Phi, are both protected natural parks. The boat stops at Koh Phi-Phi and lets off those not diving at Phi-Phi Le.

When we anchor at the beach I come up to the main deck with my waterproof camera. Twenty souls gaze out over turquoise waves, fifty yards from a virgin shore. Shimmering fish dart below the surface, some dark and solitary, some part of nervous prisms. The captain passes out snorkel masks. Someone asks if there are sharks. He says no. When he is done passing out gear the captain lowers a ladder into the water and tells everyone we have forty minutes. He says he will ring a warning bell once, then smiles and stretches his hands out towards the ocean. Everyone pretends to adjust their goggles or swim suits.

"We can just... jump in?" I ask.
"Yes, yes."

I leap. The ocean entombs me and I swim under coral reef, completely alone. A school of red and green mirror fish move through me and I ride inside their current until they shift.

I do not hear the bell, but surface to find everyone back on board. I am the last one to return. The captain slaps my back and hands me a piece of watermelon. I dangle my feet over the edge and spit seeds into the sea.

—

Down a road of ruby orchids, over a warped wooden bridge, under a trio of bent-away-from-the-ocean coconut trees, lies my Koh Phi-Phi bungalow. Ruins mark some shores, but the island is already healing. The foundations for several new buildings have been prepared. Next to my bungalow I walk by a fresh concrete slab and see someone has carved a message:

HOPE — Cowboy has been here, but will leave now because of the butterfly effect.

—

At dusk I wander the beach. Most of the shells in the bay are dark or light lavender and so the water appears a glittering periwinkle. A yellow lab follows me as I pick up shells in the shallows. The dog sniffs and sneezes at burrowing crabs. I find a perfect baby gray conch shell buried in the sand. Along the shore my flops break. I fix them with medical gauze, but they tear again within minutes. I give them a burial at sea.

So begins the era of the barefoot and the blind.

July 2nd

I sleep fourteen hours. At noon I go to the P. P. Bakery and have a breakfast of easy eggs, sausage and toast with a large pewter pot of Earl Gray. I watch 21 Grams inside the bakery and think about April.

—

In the evening I walk down the half-sand, half-brick streets with a Tiger beer in one hand and a corn on the cob in the other. I bought the Tiger beer because it had a tiger on it. I bought the corn on the cob because I liked the woman selling them. She sang corn corn corn corn on and on as she beat butter and spices over the golden cobs.

I see two Thai guys sitting at a gazebo near the sea. One of them plays guitar and they both smoke cigarettes. I sit down next to them and listen. The gentle waves tempo his six strings. After a few songs the boy playing pauses and turns to me with a question.

"Hey man... you just... eat corn and... drink beer and... walk around and sit down and listen to guitar man?"

"Yea man."

"That cool man. You so cool man."

"Thanks man."

"Hey man... you... smoke?"

"Smoke what?"

"...ganja."

"Are you a pig?"

"Pig!? I kill pig!!!"

He spits on the sand, takes out a blade and begins stabbing the air.

"Ah... okay... I believe you."

"Yea man?"

"Yea."

July 3rd

At sunrise I find a man smoking under the shade of a tree, next to three kayaks. He tells me 160 baht an hour for a one-man with free diving gear included. I push a fluorescent orange kayak into the ocean and row into the wind, away from the island. The breeze stays against me and I sweat to make pace towards the next isle. I work the oars raw until I come upon a secluded beachscape, too far away to swim to, but too small to dock at.

I row the kayak into the cove and jump out—into quicksand. I reach for a rotting log on the shore, scattering dozens of pure white and pure black butterflies. The log crumbles inside my hands as I pull myself onto solid sand. I listen to the kayak slush as I lie motionless on my back.

I stand and explore, finding a path that leads deeper, but sheets of mosquitos descend and drive me back to the open beach. They do not cross the rotting log.

When I row back I find a maze of dark reef below the surface. A shadow moves below and I feel the kayak sway. I stop paddling and wait to be tipped over.

July 4th

I e-mail everyone on the Fourth of July, then buy a pair of white flops from the dawn merchants. Tomorrow I plan on leaving Koh Phi-Phi and falling farther into the forgotten isles.

I pray to find a place the world does not remember.

—

I swim in the bay near my bungalow with borrowed goggles. I think I see a black or brown octopus in a dim cave, but do not find anything alive when I dive closer.

July 5th

I ferry to the ports of Krabi, then buy a mini-bus ticket to Trang. On a blue bus I sit next to a young woman and her baby girl. The toddler offers me some of her peanuts, then throws the rest at the driver.

At the docks in Trang I buy a ticket to Ko Mur Island. I'm the only person wanting to go anywhere at the harbor, yet less remote Ko Mur, so they put my things in a wooden long-tail boat which I must swim out into the sea to get into. As the young man and I leave I see a carnivorous crimson starfish on the shore with long black spikes sticking out over his arms.

The storms rise on the trip to Ko Mur. Winds and waves threaten to capsize us without mercy. In the midst of the elements I hear my teenage guide yelling. I thought he was going to say we had to turn back, but he points to the front of the boat, wanting me to wrap my arms around the wooden dragon. I barely stay onboard as I run to the front, throwing my arms out for the carved avatar.

I am not strapped in on a gray-green rollercoaster.

—

When we reach Ko Mur the storm has calmed and the tide is low. I jump out into a foot of ocean, less than a mile from the beach. My guide waves goodbye as I wade towards the isle. The ground moves below and I peer down to a carpet of gold starfish. Closer to the shore I start a stampede of translucent crabs who crackle and pop inside their shells as they scuttle away from my toes.

On the beach I meet a fisherwoman who tells me there is only one small village on the island and there are two bungalows and one of them has shut down. She gives me directions to the open bungalow and tells me I am the only guest on Ko Mur.

—

The Koh Mook Resort is owned by an elderly couple and kept by four young guys and three girls. Only one can speak English, a man named Cow—white in English. Cow wears a faithful black beanie that I ask to buy, but he will not sell. He gives me a key and says I don't have to pay for anything until I leave.

—

I set out southeast to map the island clockwise. As I walk the shores barefoot I find a perfect baby white conch shell and a dying man-o-war. Further on the shore turns from soft white sand into sharp black coral. The tide will soon return, but I'm close to a wall of rock and earth that offers escape. I find holes in the mountainside and try to ascend, but the coral is piercing and slick. Salt water begins to splash against my ankles, then I feel the dirt of the mountain and I pull myself above. A siren watches me, but does not smile or sing.

I start to continue forward, then notice a canyon in the coral. I peer over the edge and see a dark yellow, brown and green python, his bellying swelling with a recent meal. I take a picture, then jump over the crater. The snake does not budge from his coil.

At the end of the coral mountain I spy a narrow strip of beach with a path into the rain forest. A lonely moon illuminates specks of my path through the canopy. Gulping frogs hop over one another on the dirt road. The sounds of the true jungle fill my ears. Everywhere something comes closer, runs away, watches. A bat swoops down and all the frogs croak and scatter.

I see a flickering light through the leaves. The beacon turns into a fallen outpost with four boys gambling and drinking whisky by lantern light. They know I am lost and one young man offers to take me back to Koh Mook on his motorcycle. Thunder and rain paint our bodies as he speeds over the sand.

God is good.

July 6th

I awake to high tide at my bungalow's doorstep. After a breakfast of banana pancakes and pressed coffee I walk to the white shores of Farang Beach and the abandoned bungalow. The storms stretch with the sunrise and the waves rage. Salty wind blows sand and shells over my skin. I wade into the ocean and let the waves hurt me. After each crash I must fight not to be swept out. Soon I am exhausted and find myself unable to touch ground. I hold my lungs and dive underwater and breast stroke towards the direction of the shore. When I come back up I can stand again, but I am fifty yards from where my footprints entered. I dig myself into the sand and feel the tide foam over my feet.

—

Walking down the jungle road to Koh Mook a thin

path trails off from the flat grass. When I change courses I hear branches shake above, then a muffled huff. I look up to see a dexterous black and cream monkey following, swinging from tree to tree over my shadow.

I walk on until I uncover a crystal lagoon. The circumference is not large, but the pool appears bottomless. I'm considering diving in when a cloud of diseased mosquitos descends over me. As I'm sprinting from the lagoon I see a bright silver-blue and green snake slither across the road. He settles inside a bush next to my path. Then the monkey begins tearing bark and leaves off the trees and throwing down debris. I run forward and jump near the bush, but the snake does not strike.

Back on the main road I hear a motorcycle near and wave to the man that passes. He slows down and asks if I would like a ride back to the beach. I thank him and get on. He tells me his name is Fang, but I can call him James Bond.

In town Mr. Bond and I stop for lunch. The lone restaurant serves only rice and water. 007 speaks of the tsunami as we eat. He tells me how the wave had been as tall as a tower, how absolutely everything had been destroyed, how the land was perfectly flat afterwards.

James Bond says it was the most exciting moment of his entire life.

—

In the evening Cow invites me to eat crab with him and the guys. The legs are powerful and we must break into the jagged shells with tiny steel maces. After dinner Cow reaches into his breast pocket and takes out a green cube and a pack of bamboo papers. Blue fog floats to the rain beyond the deck and disappears.

Cow makes an animal noise and asks me if I've heard it on the island. I say no. He makes another noise. I say yes. He tells me that is a rare bird called a Hawkbill. Then he makes another noise. I say yes. He tells me that is a giant gecko. Cow says I should look for the gecko, but I will never find the Hawkbill.

July 7th

After a morning meal of leftover crab and honey/banana pancakes I set off to further explore the isle. I walk across a stone path a mile into the jungle, then a dirt road until I come to the western coasts. I climb to the top of the lonely mountain and see the Emerald Caves, then go back to Farang Beach and rest in the hammocks of the boarded-up bungalows.

At the empty resort a path of blistering sand leads back to the jungle road. As I'm walking I hear a muffled hiss from below. I look down to see my left foot standing on the head of a writhing black snake. I ponder and move away. He raises a cowled head and I see it is a baby cobra. He hisses again despite my love.

July 8th

I find the giant gecko before dawn. A proud black sack hangs from his throat. He is a just king upon his living throne. With my breakfast of pressed coffee, easy eggs and banana pancakes the girls also bring out home-battered donuts. I dip them in my coffee and watch the fishing boats come in with full nets.

I've been giving the stray bungalow dogs my scraps since I arrived and they've begun to follow me around the island because of this. Three dogs and I walk the shores after breakfast when a gray and yellow monkey appears. We chase after it until we run into a pack of wild goats. The dogs begin scattering the goats.

I run back to the coast and wade alone in the wake. I find a perfect baby peach conch shell buried in the sand. I discover hundreds of brown and white sea urchins, amber puffer-fish, black and clear aquatic centipedes, a copper sea snake and a pink crab with one fearsome claw the size of a football.

I sit in the sea and awe over the creativity of God.

July 9th

[Unknown Entry Event]

July 10th

At breakfast Cow tells me the storms are keeping the boats away from Ko Mur. They don't know when I'll be able to leave. I tell him I'm in no rush. He says that is good, but supplies will run out.

—

So I had mapped out all Ko Mur island, save the northern most shores, which were covered in sharp tawny coral that plummeted down into dire waves. I set out in early evening, accompanied by three of the dogs. On the rusted coral I must walk more carefully than on ice.

Deep into the northern shores I cross paths with a pale saltwater crocodile. He sees me after I see him and darts into the trees. The dogs run away as well, all in different directions. I am silent a moment, then press on.

After a few steps I hear rustling from the jungle. The crocodile is following me and when I turn to find him he attacks. I try to run, but slip immediately and crash onto the coral. Two streaks of dark blood trace my descent towards the suffocating waves. I dig my hands into the coral and look up. His mouth is already open.

The howls of Cerberus blare through the sea air. Three dogs streak out from the rain forest and leap in front of me, barking with reckless abandon towards the crocodile's uneven teeth. The reptile pauses, then turns and crawls back into the jungle. The dogs huddle next to me and whine as I hold my bleeding body.

I can do nothing but praise the Lord.

July 11th

My bones feel better in the morning, though I wince with every step. At breakfast they are out of eggs, milk, creme and pancake mix. Cow tells me the storms are still keeping the boats away. I will have to leave tomorrow to make my flight. After coffee and toast I go to Farang Beach. I build a grand castle with an elaborate moat, then bury myself in the broken warmth.

Before I leave I destroy the castle.

—

At dinner Cow says the boats started back this evening.

He tells me I must come back again and I tell him I will.

—

In the far ocean I wade and pray. Obsidian waves are touched by infinite galaxies and my wandering flashlight. I ask for a pure name in His book. I pray for the spirits of Solomon and Elijah. I ask for wisdom. I ask for prophecy. I ask for forgiveness.

July 12th

At the Trang Railway System I buy a second-class ticket to Bangkok that departs at two this afternoon and arrives at eight in the morning, then I walk to a computer store to send out e-mails. A Baldur's Gate box inside the store ripples nostalgia through my veins.

Thunder echoes as I run back to the railroad station in the rain. Everyone waiting for the sleeper to arrive is Thai, save one American man. He points to my cap and asks if I'm from L.A. I tell him I'm from Texas. He says I don't sound like I'm from Texas. I say I lived in Virginia some. He says he lived in Virginia a lot and all over the world. He tells me his dad was in the C.I.A. Then he asks what I'm doing in Thailand and I say just wandering around. He shakes my hand and says we are some of the last just wandering around. He tells me his name is Jim. I tell him my name is Landen. He says he likes the Dodgers and Red Sox. I say I like the

Dodgers and Rangers. I ask him what he thought about that last World Series.

Jim says it is the end of the world. I say I know.

—

On the train Jim pours us tall glasses of rum and an elderly woman grumbles as we drink. Jim says something to her in Thai and she says something back. Jim laughs, then asks me what I'm doing in Texas. I tell him I'm majoring in Creative Writing and minoring in Classics at Texas Tech. He asks me what I want to do. I tell him I want to write books. He says the world desperately needs great literature to rise again.

We lament history and future and we speak of the spiritual. Jim says he doesn't believe in God. He says religion was forced on him as a child and he feels no need to believe God exists. Jim sees my face and asks me if I believe. I say yes. He asks me what believing in God means. I say it means I know He loves me and I want to serve Him. Jim asks me if I have Peace.

I tell him I will.

V

July 13th

The streets of Bangkok flood with everlasting storms. My taxi driver floats down an alley, avoiding the sandbags and wrecks of the main streets. I feel the current rushing underneath the floorboard.

"This no taxi now," the driver says, grinning and slapping the dash. "This boat now."

—

At the Bangkok International Airport I check in and sit down at a coffee shop showing the All-Star Game. When Teixera hits a homer I look around for someone to share with, but I am the only one watching.

I am ready to be home.

July 14th

In Seoul I brush my teeth, wash my face and change into a clean gray baseball shirt.

I pray for safe passage.

I ask to share His blessings.

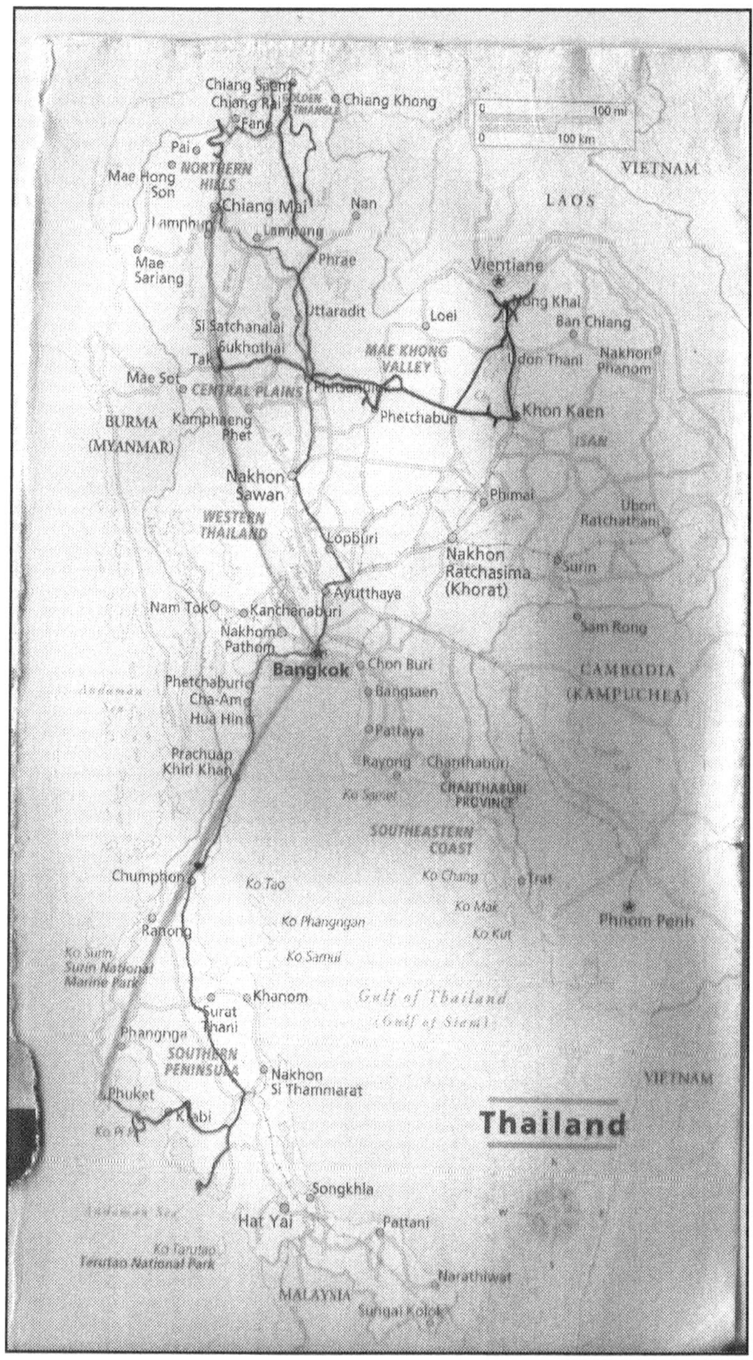

Chiang Saen
Chiang Rai
Golden Triangle
Chiang Khong
Fang
Pai
Mae Hong Son
NORTHERN HILLS
Chiang Mai
Nan
Lamphun
Lampang
Mae Sariang
Phrae
LAOS
VIETNAM
0 100 mi
0 100 km
Vientiane
Ban Chiang
Loei
Si Satchanalai
Sukhothai
Tak
MAE KHONG VALLEY
Nakhon Phanom
Mae Sot
CENTRAL PLAINS
Phetchabun
Khon Kaen
ISAN
BURMA (MYANMAR)
Kamphaeng Phet
Nakhon Sawan
Phimai
WESTERN THAILAND
Ubon Ratchathani
Lopburi
Nakhon Ratchasima (Khorat)
Surin
Ayutthaya
Nam Tok
Kanchanaburi
Nakhom Pathom
Sam Rong
Bangkok
Chon Buri
CAMBODIA (KAMPUCHEA)
Phetchaburi
Cha-Am
Bangsaen
Hua Hin
Pattaya
Prachuap Khiri Khan
Rayong
Chanthaburi
Ko Samet
CHANTHABURI PROVINCE
SOUTHEASTERN COAST
Chumphon
Ko Tao
Ko Chang
Trat
Ko Mak
Ranong
Ko Phangngan
Ko Kut
Phnom Penh
Ko Surin
Surin National Marine Park
Ko Samui
Khanom
Gulf of Thailand
(Gulf of Siam)
Surat Thani
Phangnga
SOUTHERN PENINSULA
Nakhon Si Thammarat
VIETNAM
Phuket
Krabi
Thailand
Songkhla
Hat Yai
Pattani
Ko Tarutao
Tarutao National Park
Narathiwat
MALAYSIA
Sungai Kolok

www.ingramcontent.com/pod-product-compliance
Lightning Source LLC
LaVergne TN
LVHW050943080826
845145LV00004B/1381

* 9 7 8 0 9 7 8 9 2 6 5 0 2 *